KEYBOARD HARMONY
FOR BEGINNERS

J. BARHAM JOHNSON

OXFORD UNIVERSITY PRESS
LONDON · NEW YORK · TORONTO

£2:05

OXFORD UNIVERSITY PRESS
(*Music Department*)
37 DOVER STREET, LONDON W1X 4AH

FOREWORD

FOR A GREAT many years I have taught harmony at the piano, and some hundreds of pupils have passed through my hands. I have never discovered a text-book on this subject that exactly supplies the need of the elementary pianist, or even the absolute beginner, and still less, the adult beginner. Most books assume too much knowledge, cover too much ground and cover it too quickly; the keys are not dealt with in any reasonable order, and, above all, too few exercises are provided : a pupil does not need to do one exercise twenty times, but twenty similar exercises once. The most successful text books for lower forms in subjects such as Mathematics and Latin are those in which known material is presented over and over again in different ways until it is finally assimilated.

However simply constructed, elementary pieces all contain a large proportion of common chords, with some dominant sevenths together with some kind of melodic decoration. Pieces should therefore be approached from these two directions, the harmonic and the melodic : thorough understanding of these two features will eventually ensure intelligent and fluent reading, and produce musicians.

The scope of this book is definite, though limited, and its plan is simple.

It is designed for

(1) the absolute beginner at the piano ;

(2) the elementary pianist who has never studied harmony ;

(3) pupils who have done paper work but need to put their knowledge to practical use and aural test.

The plan of the book is to treat each of five major and minor keys (up to two sharps and two flats) separately and exhaustively. Each new problem is isolated and dealt with until thoroughly known. Each set of exercises is followed by tunes, summing up the particular points studied.

The chords dealt with are Common Chords and their inversions. Dominant Sevenths are studied so far as is necessary to introduce them to a beginner.
The book ends with a few practical exercises on Melodic Decoration.

Keys are printed in the following order :

Majors—**C. G. D. F. B♭,**

Minors—**a. e. b. d. g.,**

but the exercises so designed that any reasonable order may be taken.

J. BARHAM JOHNSON

Shrewsbury School, 1946

CONTENTS

CHAPTER I

ROOT POSITIONS

Triads in a major scale are of three kinds :—
  (1) MAJOR (marked +) on Tonic, Dominant and Subdominant.
  (2) MINOR (marked –) on Submediant, Supertonic and Mediant.
  (3) DIMINISHED (marked *) on Leading note.

SCALE of C

TONIC   SUB DOMT.   DOMINANT

Preliminary exercise i. Play the chord of **C** up and down the piano in the right hand.

Note the position of the hand

  (*a*) close ;

  (*b*) 2nd finger extended (the only triad in which 2 is used) ;

  (*c*) the same position, but 3 instead of 2.

Form hand positions " in the air " before playing.

Preliminary exercise ii.   Do the same with the chord of **G**.

Preliminary exercise iii.   Up the chord of **C**, down the chord of **G**.

Also vice-versa.

PERFECT CADENCES

Formed of the chords of the Dominant to Tonic.
All exercises in this book should be played in the following way :—
  (*a*) The Left Hand plays the bass in octaves (unless the stretch is difficult for a small hand).
  (*b*) The Right Hand, keeping the melody at the top, fills in below it the next two notes of the required chord.

Notice that G is a common note.
The other notes of the two chords move *upwards*, thus :—

Whenever the melody note and the bass are the same, fingering (*b*) is required.
All these three positions should be memorized before doing the exercises.

---

†The diminished triad in root position is not dealt with in this book

Copyright, 1947, by the Oxford University Press, London.   Printed in Great Britain

ROOT POSITIONS

Preliminary exercise iv.   Up and down the chord of **F**, fingering as for **C**.

Preliminary exercise v.   Up the chord of **C**, down the chord of **F**.
Also vice-versa.

PLAGAL
CADENCES
Formed of the chords of the Subdominant and Tonic.

Notice that c is a common note.
The other notes of the two chords move *downwards*, thus :—

Whenever the melody note and the bass are the same, fingering (*b*) is required.
All these positions should be memorized before doing the exercises.

EXERCISES
On the chords of **C**, **G** and **F**.

INTRODUCING MINOR CHORDS

Preliminary exercise vi.   Up and down the piano on each of these chords,

Minor chords will be denoted by small letters in this book.

EXERCISES
On all chords learnt, filling in two inner parts. The chord to be found will always
be one of those played in the Preliminary exercises, and will always be the
chord of the left-hand note.
The inner notes should not be pencilled in, as these exercises will then lose
half their value ; but in these earlier exercises, chords may be labelled beneath,
using Capital letters for Majors and small letters for Minors.

---

†The use of the Mediant should be pointed out to pupils who do paper work.

ROOT POSITIONS

IMPERFECT CADENCES

When the music halts on the dominant.

After doing exercises 7 to 17, selected exercises should be played over to the pupil, and he should say whether Cadences are Perfect, Plagal or Imperfect.

Before the next lesson he should mark the Cadences in pencil, and this marking should be done until the Cadences are known.

SIX FRAGMENTS IN THE SCALE OF C

---

*The filling up of this progression should be shown to paper-work pupils. Also any similar progressions that may occur later.

ROOT POSITIONS

SCALE of G

The scale of **G** differs melodically from the scale of **C** in one note only. The scale of **C** has F♮, the scale of **G** has F♯

Compare the Triads in these two scales.

The following points will be noticed :—

(a) The sequence of the three types of triad is the same (and will be for every major scale).

(b) The chords of **d** and **F** are not available in **G**.

(c) Two new chords must be learnt ; **D** and **b**.

Preliminary exercise vii.   Play the chord of **D** up and down the piano.

Notice, as a guide to the eye when playing, that F♯ is successively

(a) in the middle ;

(b) at the bottom ;

(c) at the top.

Preliminary exercise viii.   Up the chord of **G**, down the chord of **D**.
Also vice-versa.

PERFECT
CADENCES

Notice that D is a common note.

PLAGAL
CADENCES

In the Plagal Cadence in **G**, both chords are common to the scale of **C**. But the Perfect Cadence introduces the distinctive semitone in the scale (F♯ to G) and is the more significant close.

ROOT POSITIONS

EXERCISES   On the chords of **G**, **D** and **C**.

INTRODUCING MINOR CHORDS

Preliminary exercise ix.   Up and down the piano on **b**.

Notice the successive positions of F♯ in the chord.

EXERCISES   On chords in the scale of **G**, introducing simple passing-notes†. Passing-notes in the melody are not " figured," but those in the bass are indicated by a dash.

IMPERFECT
CADENCES

The ear tests on these exercises and the marking of Cadences in pencil should be continued.

---

†See No. **526** (*a*) *p*. 55.

A 2

ROOT POSITIONS

SIX
FRAGMENTS IN
THE SCALE
OF G

†This Cadence can now be explained.

ROOT POSITIONS

SCALE of D

The scale of **D** differs melodically from the scale of **G** in that the scale of **G** has c♮, the scale of **D** has c♯.

Compare the Triads in these two scales.

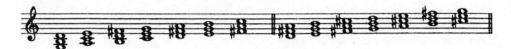

The following points will be noticed :—
  (*a*) The chords of **a** and **C** are not available in **D**.
  (*b*) Two new chords must be learnt ; **A** and **f♯**.

Preliminary exercise x. Play the chord of **A** up and down the piano (fingering as for Chord of **D**).
Notice successive positions of c♯ in the chord.

Preliminary exercise xi. Up the chord of **D**, down the chord of **A**.
And vice-versa.

PERFECT
CADENCES

Notice that A is a common note.

PLAGAL
CADENCES

EXERCISES

On the chords of **D**, **A** and **G**.

†See 526 (*d*) *p.* 55.

ROOT POSITIONS

INTRODUCING MINOR CHORDS

Preliminary exercise xii.   Up and down the piano on f♯.

Notice the successive positions of A♮ in the chord.
Here we meet, for the first time, a chord with two black notes. The thumb may be used on F♯ in the first chord.

EXERCISES   On chords in the scale of **D**.

IMPERFECT CADENCES

Continue with ear-tests and marking Cadences.

SIX FRAGMENTS IN THE SCALE OF D

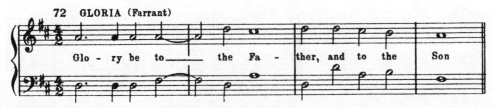

72 GLORIA (Farrant)

Glo - ry be to ____ the Fa - ther, and to the   Son

---

*See 526 (c) *p.* 55.   †See 526 (e) *p.* 55.

ROOT POSITIONS

73 JUBILATE (Aldrich)

O be joy - ful in the Lord all ye lands.

74 THIS ENDERE NYGHT

75 SARABANDE

76 PASTORAL

77 ALLELUIA

SCALE of F

The scale of **F** differs melodically from the scale of **C** in that the scale of **C** has B♮, the scale of **F** has B♭.
Compare the Triads in the two keys.

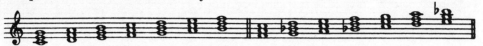

The following points will be noticed :—
  (*a*) The chords of **G** and **e** are not available in **F**.
  (*b*) Two new chords must be learnt, **B♭** and **g**.

PERFECT
CADENCES

Note that c is a common note.
Both of these chords were found in the scale of **C**, but here E is the leading note and the characteristic semitone E to F is shown.

Preliminary exercise xiii.   Up and down the chord of **B♭**.

Notice that B♭ is successively
  (*a*) at the bottom ;
  (*b*) at the top ;
  (*c*) in the middle.

PLAGAL
CADENCES

EXERCISES   On the chords of **F**, **C** and **B♭**.

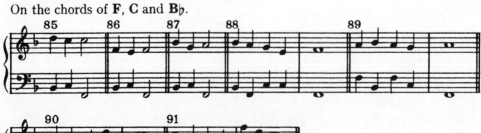

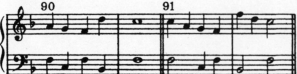

ROOT POSITIONS

INTRODUCING MINORS

Preliminary exercise xiv.   Up and down the chord of **g**.

Note, as a guide to the eye, that B♮ is successively
  (a) in the middle ;
  (b) at the bottom ;
  (c) at the top.

EXERCISES

On chords in the scale of **F**, introducing simple passing-notes. Passing-notes in
the melody are not " figured," but those in the bass are indicated by a dash.

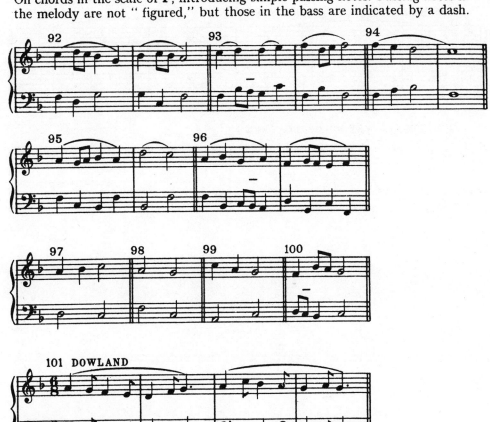

**IMPERFECT
CADENCES**

**SIX
FRAGMENTS IN
THE SCALE
OF F**

---

†Indicating a chord with a major third.

ROOT POSITIONS

103 SOURCE OF GLADNESS

104 SEELEM BRÄUTIGAN

105 ES IST EIN ROS' ENTSPRUNGEN

106 SONG OF THE VOLGA BOATMEN

ROOT POSITIONS

SCALE of B♭

The scale of **B♭** differs melodically from the scale of **F** in that the scale of **F** has E♮, the scale of **B♭** has E♭.

Compare the Triads in the two scales.

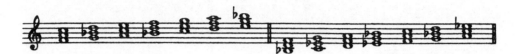

The following points will be noticed :—
  (a) The chords of **C** and **a** are not available in **B♭**.
  (b) Two new chords must be learnt ; **E♭** and **c**.

PERFECT CADENCES

Preliminary exercise xv.   Up and down the chord of **E♭**.

Notice that G♮ is successively
  (a) in the middle ;
  (b) at the bottom ;
  (c) at the top.

PLAGAL CADENCES

EXERCISES

On the chords of **B♭**, **F**, and **E♭**.

A 3

ROOT POSITIONS

INTRODUCING MINORS

Preliminary exercise xvi.   Up and down the chord of **c**.

Note that E♮ is successively
  (*a*) in the middle ;
  (*b*) at the bottom ;
  (*c*) at the top.

EXERCISES   On chords in the scale of **B♭**.

IMPERFECT
CADENCES

SIX
FRAGMENTS
ON CHORDS
IN B♭

ROOT POSITIONS

ROOT POSITIONS

ON DISCOVERING THE ROOT

Given these six chords, how is the root most quickly found?

If the chord is built up in 3rds, as at (a),
   The root is the lowest note.
   Hence, the roots are G and D.
If the interval of the fourth is present, as at (b) and (c),
   The root is the top note of the interval of the fourth.
   Hence, the roots at (b) are E and F,
      at (c) are A and G.
This method is not only useful when looking at the keyboard, but also when reading from staff notation.

These exercises are in the form of Anglican Chants, the double bar showing the two-fold nature of the chant.
The left hand should supply the root; the roots should not be pencilled in.

If these exercises are not considered sufficient, they can all be transposed into the required keys, except No. 137 which can only be transposed into **F** unless a new chord is introduced before the double bar.

ADDITIONAL
EXERCISES

In all the five keys.

†The second quaver is always a passing-note, although not shown by a dash.

ROOT POSITIONS

The same in the scale of **G**. The chord to be filled up in the Right hand.

The same in the scale of **F**.

The same in the scale of **D**.

The same in the scale of **B♭**.

1st INVERSIONS

Note

AS THE PRIMARY object of this book is to accustom the pianist to recognize and manipulate chords, without worrying him with the difficulties of correct part-writing (all of which can be learnt from a Harmony Book), he may continue to play his exercises with three notes in the Right hand and an octave in the Left. This isolates a single problem—that of discovering the correct chords in their most characteristic positions. This may result in his making consecutive octaves and fifths when two first inversions occur adjacently, because of incorrect doubling (as in Ex. 165).

To this obvious objection I would say

(1) that the pianist has only two things to avoid—the doubling of the bass of a major chord, and the doubling of the leading note in a diminished triad;

(2) that he is not held up at this stage, as are so many paper-harmonists, by academic difficulties ;

(3) that he can cover more ground in the time available.

Even the simplest pieces contain such devices as broken chords, passing notes, auxiliary notes, sevenths and pedal notes. Good reading depends so much on the quick recognition of the harmonic skeleton and on distinguishing essential from unessential notes in a melody, that an intelligent grasp of the nature of the *chords themselves* more than compensates for any lack of knowledge of the intricacies of part-writing.

But, on the other hand, pure paper work must be faultless.

CHAPTER II

FIRST INVERSIONS

The three types of Triads are shown as before.

Whereas the diminished triad is used rarely in its root position, it can be used with good effect in its first inversion.

The figure 6 is used to denote a first inversion, the other interval from the bass note being the 3rd, which, unless chromatically altered is not included in the figuring.

The quickest way to determine the name of a chord marked 6 is to think of the note in the space or line below.

It is essential, in dealing with first inversions, to recognize the three types of triad, because of " doubling ". If the chords in Chapter One have been constantly marked by the pianist with large and small letters, there should be no difficulty at this stage.

The diminished triad is the only new chord, and this will be dealt with separately.

SCALE of C

MAJOR CHORDS

As the doubling of the basses of these chords is so harsh, the following " open " positions should be memorized.

SIXTH IN THE MELODY

The easiest way to learn this position is to put down the whole four-note chord in the Right hand, and then leave out the 3rd, *i.e.*, the note played by the Bass.

PERFECT CADENCES (6th in melody)

---

†The lay-out of this chord will be referred to as the " open " position.

*All major chords will be marked by + to remind the pianist to take the " open " position. Minor chords may be " open " or " closed."

FIRST INVERSIONS

EXERCISES
(6th in melody)

THIRD IN
THE MELODY

The easiest way to learn this position is to put down triad, as at (a), and then leave out the 3rd, playing these chords in three parts only. But the " open " position, as at (b), is also available.

†PERFECT
CADENCES
(3rd in melody

PLAGAL
CADENCES

FURTHER
EXERCISES
(6th or 3rd in
melody)

⊕Here, and in similar progressions, replace the 3rd on the 3rd crotchet of the bar.
†When the Dominant or Subdominant chords are not in Root positions they are sometimes called " Inverted Cadences " (vide Bairstow). Prout does not admit them as Cadences. They are never very convincing.

FIRST INVERSIONS

THE DIMINISHED TRIAD

This is found on the note D.

Avoid doubling B, which is the leading note and has a strong upward tendency.

Good positions.

The behaviour and sound of the diminished triad must be thoroughly tested and understood. It will therefore be wise to show it in its context in some well-known passages.

The chord is marked * at each appearance.

The blank chords should be filled in by the pianist.

†See No. 526 (e) *p.* 55.   ‡See No. 526 (g) *p.* 55.

FIRST INVERSIONS

EXERCISES INCLUDING THE DIMINISHED TRIAD

THREE TUNES

FIRST INVERSIONS
SCALE of G

MAJOR CHORDS

There are now only two new chords to remember :—
  (*a*) The chord of **D** in its first inversion.
  (*b*) The diminished triad (treated later).
Since the chords of **G** and **C** in first inversions should now be well-known, only the chord of **D** major, 1st inversion, will be marked with a +

EXERCISES
(6th in melody)

FURTHER EXERCISES
(6th or 3rd in melody)

THE DIMINISHED TRIAD

FIRST INVERSIONS

The diminished triad will be marked, as before with *

EXERCISES INCLUDING THE DIMINISHED TRIAD

FOUR TUNES

FIRST INVERSIONS
SCALE of D

MAJOR
CHORDS

Only the chord of **A**, 1st inversion, will be marked with a +.

EXERCISES
(6th in melody)

FURTHER
EXERCISES
(6th or 3rd in
melody)

FIRST INVERSIONS

THE DIMINISHED TRIAD

EXERCISES INCLUDING THE DIMINISHED TRIAD

The diminished triad will be marked, as before, with *.

TWO TUNES

Preliminary exercise xvii. Up and down the chord of **E** (if this has not already been learnt when dealing with **a** minor).

FIRST INVERSIONS

PASSING SIXTH

Some preliminary practice is now required in the management of the passing sixth. The figures 5–6 generally indicate a passing sixth, when the fifth proceeds through the sixth upwards towards the next higher note. When 5–6 is in the melody there is no difficulty in seeing its behaviour.

The following examples show its use in an inner part, in the keys of **C**, **G** and **D**

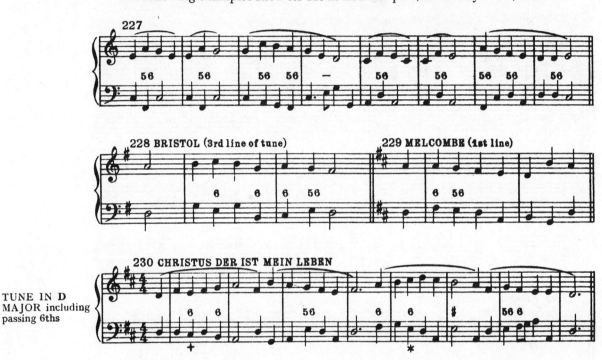

TUNE IN D MAJOR including passing 6ths

The **5–6** can be accompanied by 3–4, both the 6th and 4th being passing notes.

EXAMPLES OF 5–6 ; 3–4

FIRST INVERSIONS

SCALE of F

MAJOR CHORDS

Only the chord of B♭, 1st inversion, will be marked with a *.

EXERCISES
(6th in melody)

FURTHER EXERCISES
(3rd or 6th in melody)

FIRST INVERSIONS

THE DIMINISHED TRIAD

The diminished triad will be marked with a *.

EXERCISES
INCLUDING
THE
DIMINISHED
TRIAD

FOUR TUNES

252 I PRAISED THE EARTH

253 NAN, TELL ME TRUE

FIRST INVERSIONS

254 NORFOLK LULLABY

255 HEY NONNEY

256 O LET ME LOOK ON THEE (Lasso)

PASSING
SIXTHS

After having tried this from figured bass, the pianist may be interested to see
the actual progression of the parts at bars 3 and 4.

257

258 FOREST GREEN (1st line)

†The original starts with a bare 5th.
‡Anticipations are not figured. See No. 526 (e) p. 55.

FIRST INVERSIONS

SCALE of B♭

MAJOR
CHORDS

The chord of E♭, 1st inversion, will be marked with a +.

EXERCISES
(6th in melody)

FURTHER
EXERCISES
(6th or 3rd in
melody)

FIRST INVERSIONS

THE DIMINISHED TRIAD

The diminished triad will be marked with a *

EXERCISES INCLUDING DIMINISHED TRIAD

277 WINCHESTER NEW (1st & 3rd lines)

FIVE TUNES

FIRST INVERSIONS

CHAPTER III

SECOND INVERSIONS

SCALE of C

Used on the Dominant and Tonic.

Points to notice :—
   (a) The 6 generally proceeds to 5, and the 4 to 3, on the same bass.
   (b) The first three examples form Imperfect cadences. Should the Tonic chord follow, Full Closes would result.
   (c) The last three give a Plagal effect.
            All six examples should be memorized.
Figuring :—(a) After a Cadential $\frac{6}{4}$, the second chord is figured $\frac{5}{3}$.
            (b) The presence of the figure 4 differentiates the second inversion from the first, where 6 is accompanied by 3.
In its Cadential use, the $\frac{6}{4}$ chord falls on an accented beat† in duple or quadruple time : in triple time it may fall on the first or second beat, but may not fall on the third.

Note.—When you see the figures $\frac{6}{4}$, the chord to be played is that of the fourth above the bass.
The correct note to double is the Bass note.

---

†Because the 6 and 4 are really appoggiaturas to the 5 and 3, for this reason they are approached best by step.

SECOND INVERSIONS—CADENTIAL

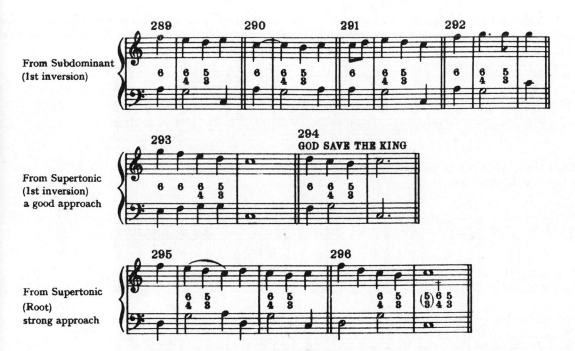

From Subdominant
(1st inversion)

From Supertonic
(1st inversion)
a good approach

From Supertonic
(Root)
strong approach

Ornamented uses of the $^6_4$ $^5_3$ may be used by the pianist in the succeeding exercises whenever the rhythm would be improved by so doing, even though such devices are not figured in exact detail.

Examples of
Ornamented uses.

HYMN TUNE

———————————————

†These really come under the heading of "pedal" $^6_4$s.
The curious effect of a succession of parallel second inversions is interesting.

"Three blind mice"

SECOND INVERSIONS—CADENTIAL

SCALE of G

I CADENTIAL

Remember the advice, when you see the figures $^6_4$, the chord to be played is that of the fourth above the Bass.

APPROACHES

HYMN TUNE

319 WORCESTERSHIRE (R.G.B. Jacob, composed 1812, aet. 11.)

SECOND INVERSIONS—CADENTIAL

SCALE of D

SECOND INVERSIONS—CADENTIAL
SCALE of F

†This is such a good example of the use of $\frac{6}{4}$ chords that it seemed worth while to figure it, in spite of bar 13 containing a chord not yet learnt. It also shows clearly how these second inversions are really all appoggiaturas.
⊕Harmonize the second quaver. See No. 526 (b) p. 55.

SECOND INVERSIONS—CADENTIAL

SCALE of B♭

SECOND INVERSIONS—PASSING

SCALE of C

II PASSING The two positions in the scale where passing $^6_4$'s are effective are

Before doing the exercises, it would be wise to see and play some examples of the passing $^6_4$ laid out in four-part vocal harmony.

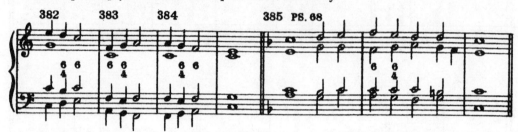

EXERCISE ON
$^6_4$ PASSING AND
CADENTIAL

Although this chord loses its chief effect when played with three notes in the Right hand and an octave in the Left, as at (a)

and is even worse at (b) where the stepwise progression of C-B-C is spoilt, yet the pianist may continue to play in this way, for his main object is the quick recognition of the notes comprising the chord. The old rule is still kept—when you see a $^6_4$. play the chord of the 4th from the Bass.

SECOND INVERSIONS—PASSING

SCALE of G

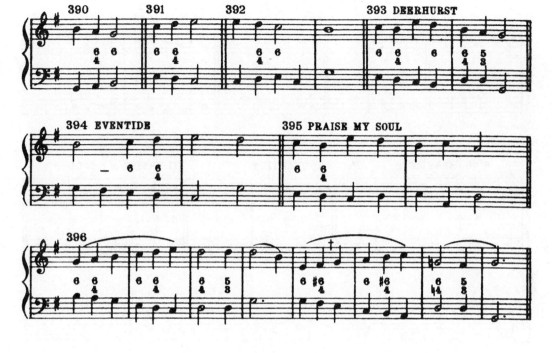

SCALE of D

---

†Unless it has already been dealt with in **e** minor, No. 443, this is a fresh chord, that of **B** major. It should be played up and down the piano, as it will be met with again in the scale of **D** which follows.

‡Unless it has already been dealt with in **b** minor, this is a new chord, that of **F♯**. It should be played up and down the piano, as shown at No. 460.

SECOND INVERSIONS—PASSING

SCALE OF F

SCALE of B♭

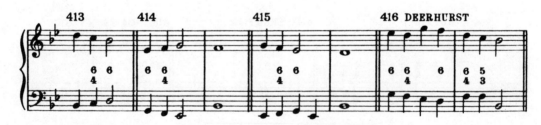

SECOND INVERSIONS—PEDAL AND GENERAL

III. ON A
PEDAL
(AUXILIARY)
Some Examples

EXERCISES on
all kinds of
6
4s

†Here an ornamental use would be appropriate.

SECOND INVERSIONS—GENERAL

CHAPTER IV
MINOR SCALES
SCALE of a minor

Triads in a minor scale are of four kinds :—
  (1) MAJOR (marked +), on Dominant and the Submediant.
  (2) MINOR (marked –), on Tonic and Subdominant.
  (3) DIMINISHED (marked *) on Supertonic and Leading note.
  (4) AUGMENTED (marked ⊕) on Mediant.

Preliminary exercise 18 (see Preliminary exercise 17, p. 36). Up and down the chord of E.

PERFECT
CADENCES

The Dominant chord is always Major, and must be shown in the figuring.

PLAGAL
CADENCES

Note.—Both chords are minor.
    If, as at (a), the last chord is major, this is called the Tierce de Picardie.
Sixteenth century writers invariably closed with a major chord.

EXERCISES on
the Chords of
a, E, d

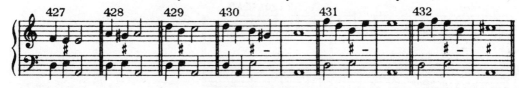

FIRST INVERSIONS IN a minor

MAJOR
CHORDS

Open positions, to be memorized.
The chord of E, 1st inversion will be marked with +.
(a) On the leading note.
    All that was said of this chord (No. 174) holds good. Avoid doubling G♯.

DIMINISHED
TRIADS

---

†This will not be dealt with in this book.

SCALE of a minor

(b) On the supertonic.

This chord, used in **a** minor, has not the same character as the same group of notes used in **C**. **B** is no longer the leading note, and has not the strong upward tendency in **a** minor.

EXERCISES ON 1ST INVERSIONS

TUNE

---

†The pianist need not worry himself over the difficulty of avoiding augmented seconds when one chord contains F and the next G♯. If he also does paper-work, then " paper " knowledge will aid his piano-playing, just as the piano sounds will aid his paper-work.

*This progression should be memorized.

SCALE of e minor

Preliminary exercise 19. Up and down the chord of **B**.

PERFECT
CADENCES

PLAGAL
CADENCES

EXERCISES on
the chords of
e, B, a

FIRST INVERSIONS IN e minor

MAJOR
CHORDS

6th at top   3rd at top

The chord of **B**, 1st inversion, will be marked with a +.

DIMINISHED
TRIADS

EXERCISES ON
1ST INVERSIONS

TUNE

†This progression should be memorized.

SCALE of b minor

Preliminary exercise. Up and down the Chord of F♯.

PERFECT AND
PLAGAL
CADENCES

EXERCISES ON
THE CHORDS
OF b, F♯, e

FIRST INVERSIONS IN b minor

MAJOR
CHORDS

6th at top   3rd at top

The Chord of F♯, 1st inversion will be marked with a +.

DIMINISHED
TRIADS

EXERCISES ON
1ST INVERSIONS

TUNE

474 TWELVE MONTHS ARE PASSED

Doloroso

SCALE of d minor

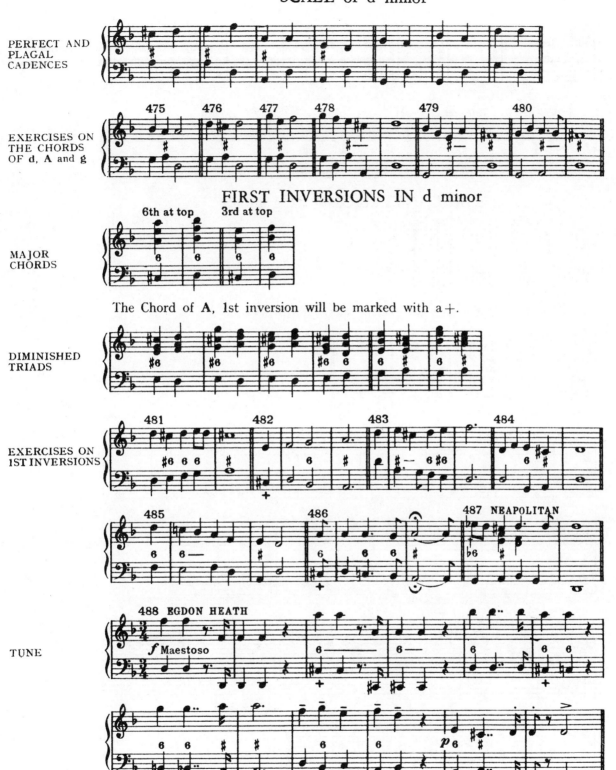

PERFECT AND PLAGAL CADENCES

EXERCISES ON THE CHORDS OF d, A and g

475 476 477 478 479 480

FIRST INVERSIONS IN d minor

6th at top 3rd at top

MAJOR CHORDS

The Chord of **A**, 1st inversion will be marked with a +.

DIMINISHED TRIADS

EXERCISES ON 1ST INVERSIONS

481 482 483 484

485 486 487 NEAPOLITAN

488 EGDON HEATH

TUNE

f Maestoso

†For E♮ chord, see No. 110 (a).

SCALE of g minor

PERFECT AND PLAGAL CADENCES

EXERCISES ON THE CHORDS OF g, D, c
489   490   491   492   493

FIRST INVERSIONS IN g minor

MAJOR CHORDS
6th at top   3rd at top

The Chord of **D**, 1st inversion will be marked with a +

DIMINISHED TRIADS

EXERCISES ON 1ST INVERSIONS
494   495

496   497

TUNE
498 SHERWOOD   simile

mp
Andante grazioso
con Ped.

cresc.

dim.

pp

SECOND INVERSIONS IN MINOR SCALES

No special exercises are needed. The pianist should play those set out for major scales, substituting in his mind the tonic minor key signature.

Note (a) all tonic chords will bear minor thirds ;
   (b) the Dominant remains major (the major third being shown in the figuring when written) ;
   (c) the approach from the Supertonic in its Root position is not available in the Minor ;
   (d) the beautiful effect of the approach from the 1st inversion of the Supertonic (which bears a diminished triad).

CHAPTER V
DOMINANT SEVENTHS

As Dominant Sevenths are found in the most elementary pieces, the beginner should know something about them. It does not lie within the scope of this book to give numerous examples of Sevenths in all possible positions, but a few practical examples will be useful.

HOW TO FORM THE DOMINANT SEVENTH

Play the Dominant of C  and add another 3rd above

This is the Dominant Seventh in C, which is a discord.
Of these notes B (the Leading note) tends to rise,
      F (the Seventh) tends to fall.

RESOLUTION

The second chord is named its " Resolution."
In the following exercises the " Resolution " will be the Tonic Chord in Root position.
There follow some examples of this chord in one or two of its most characteristic positions, those which the elementary pianist will most probably meet with very soon.

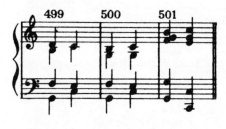

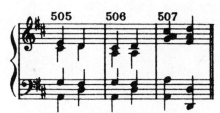
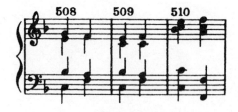

DOMINANT SEVENTHS

HOW TO
RECOGNIZE
INVERSIONS

1st Inv. 2nd Inv. 3rd Inv.

Each chord contains the interval of the second, which we will call " the smudge ".

The Dominant note is always the upper note of the " smudge." The Seventh is always the lower note of the " smudge."

Find the Dominant of the following chords by the method suggested. Play the Dominant note in octaves in the left hand, and discover the best " resolution " (some position of the Tonic).

Example. 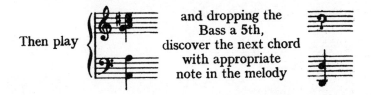 being given, the top note of the " smudge " (A) is the note for the Left hand.

Then play 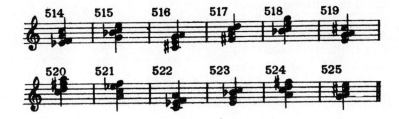 and dropping the Bass a 5th, discover the next chord with appropriate note in the melody

EXAMPLES

514   515   516   517   518   519

520   521   522   523   524   525

CHAPTER VI

MELODIC DECORATION

The quick recognition of Chords is one of the chief factors in promoting good reading. With this knowledge as a basis we can go a step further.

Few melodies are altogether without decoration. When once the " harmony notes " of a melody are discovered, we can see where the decoration lies.

By " harmony notes " is meant the notes in the melody belonging to the supporting chord. Decorative notes are all those which are not " harmony notes ".

Examine the following passage from Mozart's Sonata in C (K. 545)† and see how the melody, when looked on from a harmonic point of view, loses much of its difficulty. The harmony is shown by the figuring.

(Slow movement, bar 7.)

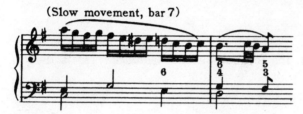

If we take out all decoration notes, the result will be

a very simple piece of three-part writing.

Notice that decoration consists in taking notes *adjacent* to a Harmony-note.

THIS IS THE PRINCIPLE OF ALL DECORATION.

Again, consider this simple fragment of harmony

and see how, in bar 17 of the same movement, Mozart has added decoration.

---

†Examples are purposely taken from the two Sonatas which are so often tackled by elementary pianists.

‡The c♯ is a passing note, leading to B on the next beat.

MELODIC DECORATION

Again, consider this simple harmony :—

The key at the moment is **g** minor, and the harmony not outside the scope of this book, being all common Chords.

In the same Sonata Mozart has ornamented the passage in this way :—

Again, consider this fragment of harmony :—

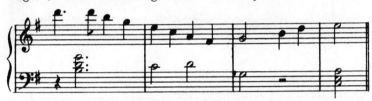

Beethoven in his Op. 49, No. 2, has decorated it in this way :—

526

METHODS OF DECORATION

Melodic Decoration is brought about by :—
    (*a*) Unaccented passing notes.
    (*b*) Accented passing notes.
    (*c*) Auxiliary notes proper.
    (*d*) Appoggiaturas.
    (*e*) Anticipatory notes.
These are the chief devices, all using " adjacent " notes :—
    (*f*) Such ornaments as the turn
    (*g*)   or the trill
        are compounded of harmony notes and notes adjacent to them.

†No. 526 (*b*).   ‡No. 526 (*f*).

MELODIC DECORATION

The following exercises are designed for more advanced pianists to put into practice the adding of melodic decoration to a tune.

The portion in square brackets shows the decoration in full, but after that the melody is shown unadorned. The type of decoration shown under the square bracket should be added at the places considered most suitable : there may be various solutions. Exercises may be played several times, with decorations varied in place and in type. Rhythmic considerations should guard against the excessive use of ornamentation.

Unless otherwise directed, play only the melodic line in the R.H.

MELODIC DECORATION

531 Play R.H. according to the figuring, with added ornament: L.H. in 8ves

Molto sostenuto

532

Tempo di Gavotta

533 Play in Chords in both hands

534

535

MELODIC DECORATION

MELODIC DECORATION

542 Left hand devises an accompaniment with the help of the figures

Play also with chords in R.H., and 8ves in L.H.

543

Play in two parts only. After playing, write out the best solution, and choose suitable fingering. Transpose it then into F and alter the fingering to suit that key. cp. "Early One Morning."

544

Reproduced and printed by
Halstan & Co. Ltd., Amersham, Bucks., England